How We Get Our Mail

By Edith S. McCall

Pictures — Lucy and John Hawkinson

BENEFIC PRESS · CHICAGO

Publishing Division of Beckley-Cardy Company

Atlanta 3, Georgia
Long Beach 3, California

Dallas 1, Texas
Portland 4, Oregon

Supplementary
Social Studies Program

Photographs furnished by:
Dorothy Reed, Chicago

How Series

HOW HOSPITALS HELP US
HOW SCHOOLS HELP US
HOW WE CELEBRATE OUR SPRING HOLIDAYS
HOW WE GET OUR MAIL

HOW AIRPLANES HELP US
HOW WE CELEBRATE OUR FALL HOLIDAYS
HOW WE GET OUR CLOTHING
HOW WE TRAVEL ON WATER

HOW WE GET OUR CLOTH
HOW WE GET OUR SHELTER
HOW WE TRAVEL ON LAND

Library of Congress
Number 60-6591

Basic Concepts Series

HOW MAPS AND GLOBES HELP US
HOW PEOPLE LIVE IN THE MIDDLE EAST

A letter dropped in the corner mailbox or at the post office passes through many hands and many processes before it reaches its destination. Mailmen picking up mail at corner boxes, workers at the post office windows, mail sorters, those who bag mail, and those who carry mail on local delivery trucks, highway mail trucks, trains, ships, and airplanes all work together to bring our mail to us.

CONTENTS

MAIL ON THE WAY

Letters, letters, letters.

Letters, letters, letters.
Into the mailbox go many letters.

Soon a man from the post office comes
in a truck.

He stops the truck near the mailbox.

The man has a big bag.

He takes all the letters from the box.

Then into the big bag go the letters.

The man puts the bag into the truck.

He goes up one street and down the other,
from mailbox to mailbox.

He takes letters from many boxes,
and puts them into his big bags.

Then away he goes to the post office.

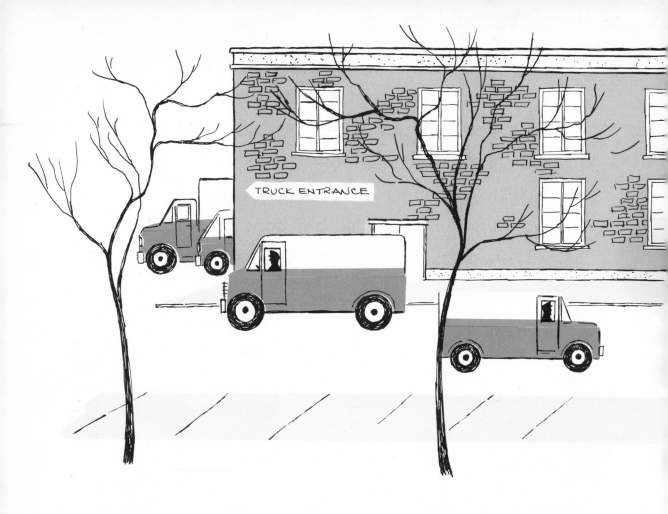

Many other men in trucks help to take mail
to the post office, too.

TO THE POST OFFICE

The men in trucks do not pick up all the mail.

Some people do not put their letters into mailboxes.

They do not have stamps for their letters.

They go to the post office to buy stamps.

Some people have packages to mail.

Their packages are too big for the mailbox.

They take their packages to the post office.

This man wants his letter
to go fast.

He goes to the post office
to buy a stamp like this.

Air mail stamp

Now his letter will go in an airplane.

This boy wants a
stamp like this.

Special delivery stamp

Now his letter to Bill Brown
will go fast.
When his letter gets
to Falls City, it will not go
out with the other letters.
It will go right to Bill.

11

This girl goes to the post office.

She has a big package to mail.

The post office worker tells her how many stamps she must buy to mail the package.

Then he puts stamps on the package.

Now the package is on its way.

It will go by truck or by train.

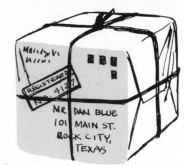

This package must not be lost.
A very good ring is in the package.
The package is marked and stamped
like this.

The mailman in Rock City will take
the package to Dan Blue.

Dan Blue must put his name
on a paper.

Then the mailman will give Dan
the package.

This is what the mailman must do
with packages like this.

POST OFFICES, BIG AND SMALL

This is where the men in the trucks go
with the letters from the mailboxes.
This is a big post office.
Many people come here every day.

But a post office can be very small like this one.

People in a small town like to go to the post office.

They get their mail and see each other.

15

A post office can be very, very big.
This is a big city post office.
Trucks and trains go under it.

16

Each post office has a postmaster.
This is a postmaster at work.

This postmaster works
in a small post office.
   She does not have much help
with the post office work.

In a very big city post office the postmaster has many, many workers to help with the mail.

WORK WITH THE MAIL

Letters picked up from mailboxes come into the post office.

People come to the post office with mail.

But there is more mail on its way.

Every day workers from big companies take letters to the post office.

Many companies have packages to mail, too.

Men in big trucks take the packages to the post office.

Letters and packages from many
companies are stamped.

These companies have a machine
like this to stamp letters.

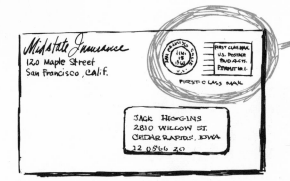

The machine makes stamps
to put on packages, too.

In the big city post office,
the bags of mail go for a ride.
The letters come out of the bags.
Down they go to the workers.
The workers are ready for them.

Small letters go together,

and big letters go together.

The post office worker must see
the stamps on the letters.
Then the letters go through a machine.

The machine marks the stamp like this.
This stamp cannot be used again.

Cancellation marks

Postmark

The machine puts a postmark
on each letter, too.

The postmark tells where the letter
was mailed.

It tells when the letter was mailed, too.

Each post office has a postmark.

Workers read to see where each
letter is going.

All letters going to one place
are put together.

Now the letters are ready to go
into bags again.

These bags will go to other post offices.

Some of the big post offices will get
much mail.

There is a bag for each of these
big post offices.

Mail for small towns near by is
put together in one bag.

Workers on the trains and trucks will
see that each small town gets its letters.

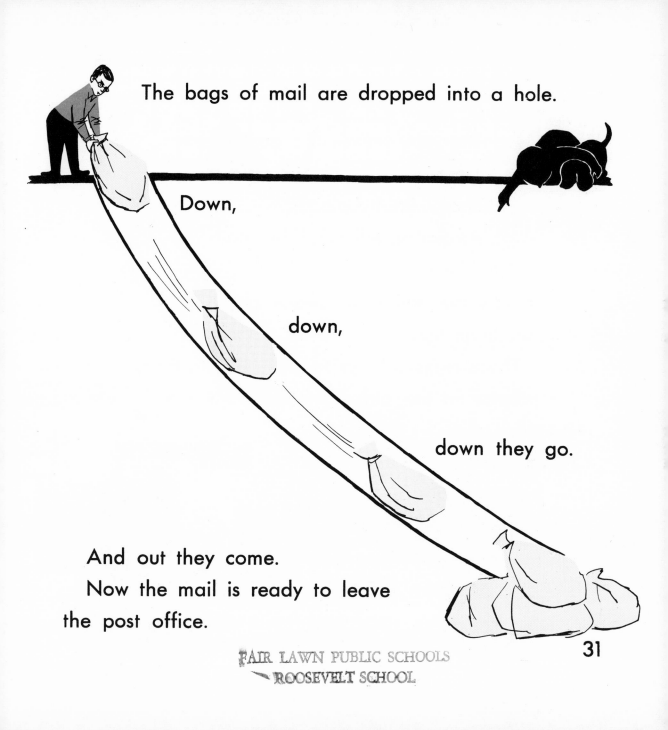

The bags of mail are dropped into a hole.

Down,

down,

down they go.

And out they come.
Now the mail is ready to leave
the post office.

POST OFFICES THAT MOVE

The mail leaves the post office.
Trucks and trains will take it
to many, many places.
    Airplanes will take the mail
that must go fast.
    Ships will help take the mail, too.

UNITED STATES POST OFFICE

33

This is a post office, too.

It is the post office on a train.

As the train goes along, workers take
mail out of some of the bags.

They get the mail ready to leave
the train.

Others work with the mail that comes
onto the train.

The train does not stop
at many small towns.
But the train drops
and picks up bags of mail.
This is how a bag is
dropped while the train moves.

This is how a bag is picked
up while the train moves.

Some trucks are post offices that move, too.
They go to many post offices
to pick up and leave mail.

Inside a highway
post office truck

This airplane takes mail, too.

Some airplanes are post offices that move.

Others are not, but they help to take the mail fast.

THE MAIL COMES IN

Trucks and trains, airplanes and ships---
They all work together to take the mail
to other post offices.

There is much work to do when the mail
gets to all the post offices.

Here comes the mail into a big city post office.

Many boxes and bags of mail have come.

Some will go to people in the big city.

Some mail will stay in the post office.
People will come in and ask for it.
Other mail will go on to small post offices.
The mail goes up into the post office.
The workers are ready for it.

A big city is marked out in zones like this.

Zone 5

The zone mark tells a post office worker where a letter is to go in the city.

This mark helps him put the letter with others going to the same zone.

Then other workers get the mail ready for the mailmen in each zone.

They put all the mail for each mailman into one place.

Zone number

42

THE MAIL GOES OUT

Then each mailman gets his mail ready
to go into his bag.

Mailman's
route case

He puts all the letters for each
street together.

Then he puts the letters into his bag.

Now the mailman is ready to leave
the post office.

43

Many times a mailman has too
much mail for his bag.

The mail he cannot take will
be put into trucks.

These trucks will take the
mail to a box like this.

As the mailman comes to a box,
he takes out the mail.

He puts the mail into his bag and
takes it on to the right places.

To get the mail to us, the mailman can go---

in a car,

or in this.

But many mailmen walk.
They walk, and walk, and walk.
They walk when it rains.
They walk when it snows.
They bring the mail to us!

45

Many people work together---

46

---to bring the mail to us.

Vocabulary

The total vocabulary of this book is 142 words. Of these, 42 are first-grade, 15 are above first-grade level, and the rest are below this level. First-grade words are listed in roman type, and italics are used for words above first-grade level. The words are listed in alphabetical order, and the numbers indicate the the pages on which the words first appear.

airplane 10
along 34

bag 6
bring 47
buy 9

city 16
companies 22

does 19
dropped 31

each 15

goes 7

hole 31

its 12

leave 31
letters 4
lost 13

machine 23
mail 4
mailbox 5
mailman 13
many 5
marked 13
men 8
more 22
move 32
much 19

near 6

office 6
other 7

packages 9
paper 13
people 9
pick 9
place 28
post 6
postmark 27
postmaster 18

rains 45
ring 13

ships 32
small 14
snows 45
some 9

stamps 9
stay 41
street 7

their 9
these 23
through 26
together 26
town 15
train 12
truck 6

very 13

worker 12
while 36

zones 42